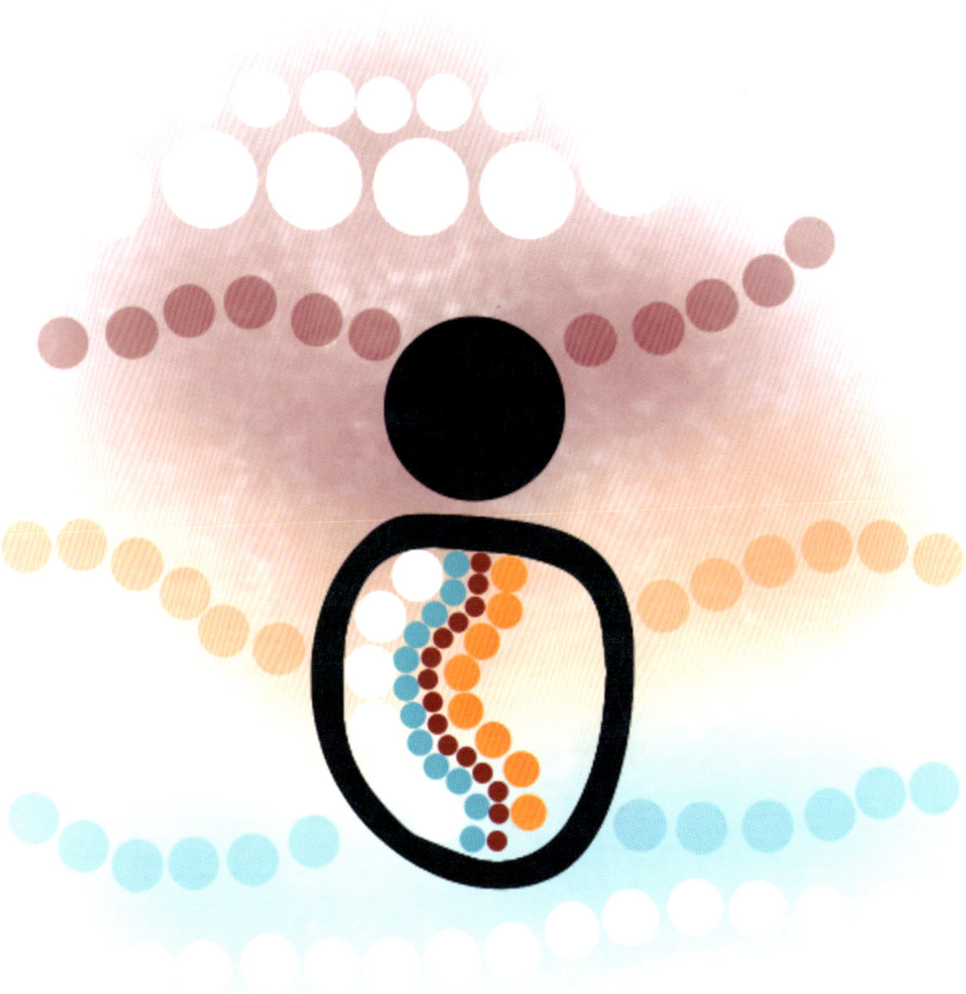

AF584009

Hi, my name is Krystal Randall. My Mum is a Yaegl woman and my Dad is a Bundjalung man. I grew up with my FAMILY in a place called Malabugilmah Village. It's a small Aboriginal community about an hour from Grafton. It's located in the beautiful Northern Rivers area of New South Wales.

family

During my childhood, we would go hunting and swimming with our Pop every weekend. He taught us how to gather wild honey from the bush and how to dive for turtles. He would help us to catch goannas and seek out echidnas. He would even show us how to find witchety grubs in trees. On the way, Pop used to sing little songs in language. We always had so much FUN.

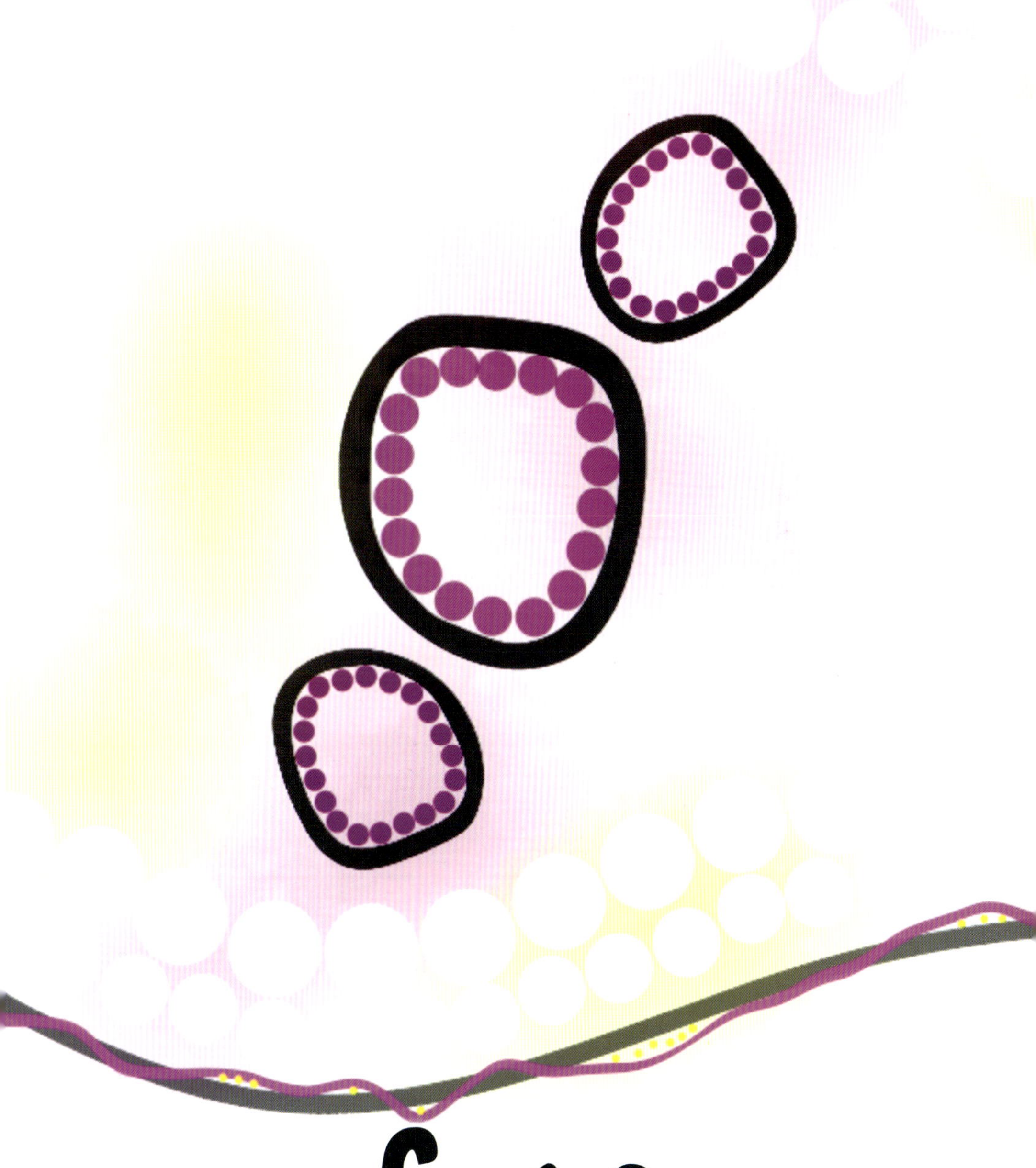

fun

Pop was very WISE. He taught us so much about connecting to the land and to our culture. As an adult, I still cherish the lessons he taught me.

wise

I feel like everyone needs to have that connection to something they love or are passionate about. I love connecting to my culture and sharing it with others. I feel proud and full of HOPE when I see it passed onto younger people.

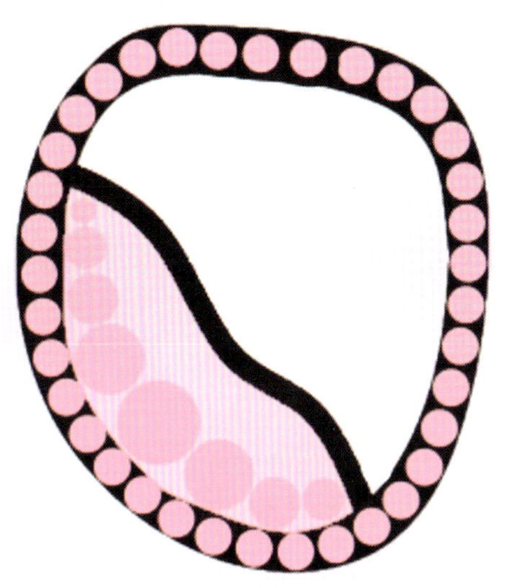

hope

One of the ways I like to connect to my culture is through painting. I love to paint on really big canvasses. I love to tell stories through my artwork. A few years ago, I started playing with digital art. I love the neverending colour choices and I love being CREATIVE with my computer.

creative

I work with high school students. One thing I've noticed is that some students have difficulty communicating with others. I really wanted to be HELPFUL and make a difference in their lives. I realised that I could do this through my passion for digital art. This is how the idea of my Yarn Circles Wellbeing Cards came about!

helpful

My Yarn Cards help those students who really don't feel like talking or expressing their emotions. They can pick out a card that best describes how they're feeling, like this SAD card. It allows them to knock down their walls and open up about their feelings. It helps them to move past bad things and focus on good things.

sad

I use my Yarn Cards with students in traditional Yarning Circles. Yarn time was a really important way for our First Nations ancestors to communicate and connect with their people. This ancient practice of SHARING thoughts and feelings is still working today!

sharing

One of my favourite Yarn Cards is BELONG. Everyone needs to feel a sense of belonging. This can be with your family, or friends or a group. The feeling you get from belonging to someone, or something, is very special.